I am forgiven

Zithini Dlamini

ISBN: 1492932019
ISBN 13: 9781492932017
Library of Congress Control Number: 2013919328
CreateSpace Independent Publishing Platform
North Charleston, South Carolina

Contents

Preface

What's Special about the Book?

GOD is in the business of forgiving us every day. His eye is constantly on the lookout, depositing seeds of forgiveness in our hearts. All we need to do is nurture them and allow them to bear fruit. He purposes to do this so that we can become effective in the house of GOD or toward the calling He has for each one of us.

The book looks at the life of born-again children of GOD and how they deal with issues of unforgiveness. Just because you are a Christian doesn't mean that your heart won't be broken or that you won't break other people's hearts. What happens when you find it hard to forgive—especially when these people are your family, fellow church members, flat mate, colleagues, etc.? These people are constantly in your face. Instead of forgiving them, your anger is kindled, and you grow to hate them and feel justified in that hatred. Remember you are a child of GOD. Shouldn't forgiveness come naturally to you? We are quick to quote this verse to others (forgive their trespasses as we forgive those who trespass against us), but when it's our turn to put it into practice, we find it difficult. What prevents us from forgiving others? *I Am Forgiven* will expose you to the day-to-day challenges that can easily result in unforgiveness when left unattended. You need this book to win the battle so that you can also go and tell someone else: *I Am Forgiven.*

Aim of This Book

The title reads "I Am Forgiven." This person is someone who is a Christian, someone who is born-again but missed it along the way. In spite of all the wrongs we have committed, GOD has forgiven all wrongdoing.

We look at the life of a forgiven Christian. What does it mean? Are there any lessons to help newborn Christians?

The book does not offer solutions but guidelines.

You can stay out of sin for good—it's a choice.

Nobody needs forgiveness as much as a person who is born-again, since judgment will begin in the house of the LORD. Forgiveness is for oneself and for others.

About the Author

Zithini Dlamini was a field and studio presenter for the South African Police Services—Police File program, which is featured on SABC 2.

Zithini Dlamini has written a number of articles on crime incidents and land reform matters, which received national coverage on newspapers and magazines.

Over the years, she has produced a number of newsletters for the Department of Rural Development and Land Reform as the editor from 2007 to 2010.

This is Zithini Dlamini's first book. The cases discussed are not imagined but real experiences; some are intensely personal.

Introduction

I Am Forgiven

(To rise above all my daily struggles)

I can't even remember the exact day I was saved or the year, but I believe that I have been saved for twelve years now.

It has been very challenging for me -, and along the journey mind-blowing too on the other hand.

I went to church in Nelspruit, the church I have embraced ever since I started working here. Some of the things they do at Word of Grace remind me of my home church—Church on a Mission.

Just after we finished praise and worship, I sat down, and I heard a voice clearly saying to me I should write a book with the title "I am forgiven." That was six years ago.

My eyes filled with tears, as I could not comprehend why GOD would entrust me with such a huge task. I thought of all the wrongs I have done and was overwhelmed with GOD's love for me. How does He keep loving past my failures? I never thought this kind of love existed.

I'm experiencing GOD's personal love for me. Can you believe it? Yes, *I Am Forgiven*—for Jesus took away *all* my sins when He died on the cross for me.

I am forgiven; I am free; I am born-again

Prelude

Colossians 3: 8–17 (NLT)

But now is the time to get rid of anger, rage, malicious behavior, slander, and dirty language. Don't lie to each other, for you have stripped off your old sinful nature and all its wicked deeds. Put on your new nature, and be renewed as you learn to know your Creator and become like Him. In this new life, it doesn't matter if you are a Jew or a Gentile, circumcised or uncircumcised, barbaric, uncivilized, slave, or free. Christ is all that matters, and He lives in all of us.

Since GOD chose you to be the holy people He loves, you must clothe yourselves with tender-hearted mercy, kindness, humility, gentleness, and patience. Make allowance for each other's faults, and forgive anyone who offends you. Remember, the Lord forgave you, so you must forgive others. Above all, clothe yourselves with love, which binds us all together in perfect harmony. And let the peace that comes from Christ rule in your hearts. For as members of one body you are called to live in peace. And always be thankful.

Let the message about Christ, in all its richness, fill your lives. Teach and counsel each other with all the wisdom He gives. Sing psalms and hymns and spiritual songs to GOD with thankful hearts. And whatever you do or say, do it as a representative of the Lord Jesus, giving thanks through Him to GOD the Father.

one

Who Is in the Church?

Do you know who is in the church today? The church is filled with people who are divorced or going through divorce; separated or going through separation; widowed and forgotten; sick and alone; people who abuse substances and are ashamed of it; women-bashers and the women they shame; children born out of wedlock who are stigmatized; men and women who practice witchcraft and have been in the church for years unnoticed; couples who stay together but are not married; child molesters and fraudsters; and so on.

Each one of these people has a story to tell. They want to be heard; they wish for someone to listen to their shame, someone to tell them that there is still hope. They all know that the church is a place of refuge, but something is not right.

When an altar call is made, they don't go in front to be prayed for. After all, everybody thinks they are holier than thou. They have the appearance of saints, people who can never do wrong.

They are seen as pillars of the church: they are elected to high positions in the church. Nobody suspects them of any wrongdoing. Honestly, nobody can associate them with any wrongdoing. They are regarded as "good examples." New converts look up to them, and they even consult them in confidence on personal matters. They have earned the trust of most church members, including the pastor.

But they are leaking wounds—gaping wounds of sin. This is the church today: a church of born-again Christians. Some of them are unashamed and daring. They continue to think that they can never get caught, since they are born-again. They proclaim boldly that their sins are forgiven. They say that they are washed in the blood of Jesus. Are they?

...scarred, yet still in the church

The irony in this is that the offender and the victim are both in the church—not necessarily in the same building, but they are both in the church. They are both continuing to serve GOD. They claim that they love the LORD with all their hearts. The offender is putting on a face, a mask that church members can't see through. They smile at you, but someone is crying because of them, spending sleepless nights because of them. You don't see it. Worse still, you don't suspect any wrongdoing.

Now, these poor victims, where can they run to? Who will believe them? This is wrong, so very wrong.

But...

GOD sees all this—GOD sees everything.

Every day we are surrounded by these people. They are all around us. We come into contact with people who are leaking wounds, but we don't see that. We are all busy, busy with our day-to-day issues. We are too busy to listen, to care, to pay a visit, to call—too busy to notice.

But...

GOD goes about planting seeds of forgiveness in the hearts of us all—those we label wicked and good alike. He tells me and you every day to go out and forgive.

two

Is There Any Hope?

From generation to generation, everyone knows that the church is a place of refuge. We go there to meet GOD. We go there to change, because we desire to change.

When the church is filled with the kind of people described in the first chapter, is it still safe? Let me answer by saying that, without a doubt, the church is a safe place—our refuge.

Have you ever asked yourself why these people continue to come to church? What do they hope to find? They are messed up, and they continue to mess other people. Do they get any joy from seeing people become miserable? Why can't GOD wipe them from the planet? Surely we don't need them.

Hold it right there; let us not forget that we are living in a time of grace, GOD's abundant grace upon humankind. Jesus's heart is crying out for each one of us. It tells us to repent!

GOD is reaching out to those people sitting in church, and He says repent from all your wrongdoing. The ONE who is able to convict a human heart, since He made it, is reaching out to them, one by one, and repeating the same message: *repent*. GOD is reaching out to both the offender and the victim. He wants to heal them both.

Within the makeup of every human being, there is a deeper longing for GOD. Something inside of us longs to connect with GOD, no matter who you are. In fact, 99 percent of human beings start out at church, whether born-again or not. Our existence is molded by GOD. You may not like to hear it if you have backslidden or have denounced GOD, but you know very well this is the truth.

Since you are still alive, GOD has not given up on you. He wants you back. Can you help me?

Being in the church is not only about singing praises and dancing. The church today is dealing with a lot. It is dealing with personalities—people who come every day seeking solutions and answers. The church is not just the structure but the people in it.

We all have an obligation to present the true church to others. People are going around every day seeking, hoping to find the true church.

Let us look at this scripture from Ephesians 4:11–16 (NKJV):

> And He Himself gave some to be apostles, some prophets, some evangelists, and some pastors and teachers, for the equipping of the saints for the work of ministry, for the edifying of the body of Christ, till we all come to the unity of the faith and of the knowledge of the Son of GOD, to a perfect man, to the measure of the stature of the fullness of Christ; that we should no longer be children, tossed to and fro and carried about with every wind of doctrine, by the trickery of men, in the cunning craftiness of deceitful plotting, but, speaking the truth in love, may grow up in all things into Him who is the head; Christ; from whom the whole body, joined and knit together by what every joint supplies, according to the effective working by which every part does its share, causes growth of the body for the edifying of itself in love.

An extract from (Hebron's Mexico Missions. "Equipping Faithful Disciples" Who should be equipped for ministry? Accessed July 13, 2013. http://www.equipsaints.org/equip1.htm) best explains the passage above. It reads: "The history of the Church is *not* the story of the shining lights, the big voices, the ones who preached to thousands; it's the story of the saints being equipped and doing the work of the ministry." ()

One other example comes from Flavil R. Yeakley Jr in Why Churches Grow. In his book Yeakley emphasized the importance of every member getting involved in some way or another.

- "The more involved a person becomes in the work of the congregation, the more important the congregation becomes in his life. It logically follows, therefore, that a congregation which offers people many opportunities for involvement would be more successful in attracting and keeping converts than would a congregation which offers few opportunities for involvement." (Yeakley, 1979,40)

- "Total evangelism includes more than reaching the lost. It also includes involving the members in the work of the local congregation. If a congregation does not use its members it loses them...the congregations with the highest dropout rate were the congregations with the lowest involvement level." (Yeakley, 1979,113–114)

- "If a congregation can maintain a high involvement level, its conversion rate will be higher, its dropout rate will be lower, and thus its net growth rate will be higher." (Yeakley, 1979, 44–45) ()

Can the church count on you? Will you serve GOD with the gifts that He has bestowed upon you? Will you make yourself available?

Now, more than ever before, the church requires the saints to get to work. Are you willing to discover the purpose of your existence? It's not enough that you wake up every day to go to work and come back to your family. You go to school and back. This is routine—what about discovering your real potential? There's a lot within you.

Can we get started?

GOD wants to equip us with His Word so "that we should no longer be children, tossed to and fro and carried about with every wind of doctrine, by the trickery of men, in the cunning craftiness of deceitful plotting" (Ephesians 4:14-15 NKJV)

three

Going for Surgery

Let us go back to the people who are in the church. Some come with leaking wounds, and they look really bad. The church whisks them into theater to perform a surgery of repentance and restoration. Now, this is what happens in the surgical theater:

A week or so before surgery, the doctor or nurse will often tell you to avoid certain foods and stop taking supplements (even herbal). On the day before surgery, they tell you not to eat at all. Sometimes you are not even allowed to drink liquid. Your body gets prepared for what is to come.

The same thing happens to us. GOD will tell you to go on a fast. You are not allowed to take any form of food; or perhaps you may consume only one kind of food. This is preparation—preparation for restoration, because GOD knows that flesh and blood *cannot* inherit the things of GOD but the Spirit. "What I am saying dear brothers and sisters, is that our physical bodies cannot inherit the Kingdom of GOD. These dying bodies cannot inherit what will last forever." (1Corinthians 15:50 NLT)

Now when you are prepared for surgery, sometimes you are made to fill in some form that says, "In the event you don't make it, the doctors cannot be held responsible." Even the doctors understand that they can *only* do so much. *Only* GOD can attend to the spiritual, since He is the Great Physician. There are certain operations, right in the middle of your operation, that are not performed by human hands but by GOD *alone*.

So He lets you sign the consent forms, because He already knows how it will turn out. Will you trust Him?

You lie there thinking: *What if I don't make it?* But something inside you tells you that it's going to be all right. It's like someone is whispering words into your ears that no one else can hear. So, you take the pen and give consent.

You are whisked into theater, and minutes later you are unconscious. You don't know what is happening to you. You can't see it, because GOD put Adam to sleep when He created Eve. GOD would not have allowed Adam to be so terrified that he would have run away at the sight of his rib being removed from him. Fear would have gotten the grip of him and told him to run, outweighing his trust in GOD. A human being's first reaction when faced with a scary situation is to flee or fight. Adam would have wanted to do the same. So GOD, in His infinite wisdom, put Adam to sleep. The same thing happens in the surgical theater: you are put to sleep so that when you wake up, you can marvel with joy.

They strip off your clothes and dress you in a hospital gown. When GOD is dealing with you, He strips off all the makeup and the masks that you have put on. He needs to see clearly so that He cannot miss any spot; even the one you thought was minor. GOD attends to all of them—one-by-one. He lays you bare. He turns the light of the theater to shine bright on the spot. First, the doctor cleans the wound to remove all dirt. Then the surgeon comes in to start with the operation. The surgeon is putting you back together again, into the right shape—because GOD wants to see you perfect, since He is also perfect.

This takes place in quiet, the only time they talk is when the surgeon talks to the nurse or team. It stays quiet, right until the end. Surgery demands total focus and concentration, because any form of distraction might result in a botched surgery. The doctor takes great care.

Now, can you see that even without going into surgery, but the blood of Jesus does the same thing for you: it washes all sin and impurities in your system. You don't get to see it with your physical eye, just like the person who is being operated on—but the Lord will be busy at work in you, fixing every part that is not right in you. He wants to see you in your perfect shape. GOD does not delight in imperfection at all, because you are His workmanship, created in Christ Jesus unto good works that GOD had predestined that you should walk in them. So when you find yourself separated, be grateful you are under construction, away from all the noise and disturbances.

When the operation is over, you are helped on a trolley and wheeled into the recovery room. Nursing staff will watch you closely for at least half an hour as you recover from your anesthetic to ensure you are safe and free from pain and nausea. When they are satisfied with your condition, you will be moved either to the ward, if you are staying, or the day surgery recovery area if you are leaving.

Here's what GOD wants you to know—His after-care is endless.

four

Forgiveness Must Be Spoken Before It Can Be Felt: You Need the Word

Over and above everything else you have read about forgiveness, I want you to understand that forgiveness is a state of mind, a mind that has been released to prosper, a mind that has been held captive for too long.

A mind that says now "I can do *all things* through Christ who strengthens me."

But

It begins with spoken words.
The principle is the same for believers and nonbelievers.
Let's read Genesis 1:1: "In the beginning God created the heaven and the earth. And the earth was without form, and void; and darkness was upon the face of the deep. And the Spirit of God moved upon the face of the waters. And God said, Let there be light: and there was light."

GOD spoke it into being. Had GOD not spoken, nothing would have happened. GOD spoke it, and He saw it. Words create, and they also rearrange and put things in the right order.

You will never experience forgiveness until your mind feels liberated. Hearing the words "You are forgiven" will liberate the mind, the mind that was in darkness now begins to see the light.

For if your mind stays trapped, it becomes the devil's playground: to manipulate, deceive, and connive to cause you not to forgive. Get out!

He has held you for too long, blinded by unforgiveness.

...You need the word.

This book is titled *"I Am Forgiven."* This is a statement that is spoken by someone who holds the power—the power to forgive.

In this book we're not talking about any ordinary being but GOD himself who gave me the title. He told me to write this book, just as He told me I'm forgiven.

It is important for us to see that until these words are spoken in our lives, we remain slaves. Spoken words carry the power to liberate.

Have you ever heard Christians talking/praying and saying, "Lord, we need a word from you"? As human beings, we realize that unless words are spoken, we remain in the same position that we've always been.

Another example is when couples fight and one of them says: "I want to hear you say it. Tell me you don't love me anymore; tell me!" Even though the signs might be there, it must first be spoken before it can register in our minds.

The principle is the same, even for nonbelievers. It takes sweet words for a girl to fall in love with a boy before any action can be taken. The genesis of it comes from spoken words. The opposite is also true when a person says, "I hate you." Words first need to be registered in your mind before any action can be taken.

This is the power of spoken words.

So you see, when GOD says you are forgiven, it simply means this is a carefully thought out plan. He says: "I know what I'm doing, and, as a result, I choose to forgive you."

five

What Should My Reaction Be?

After the warm feeling and excitement have died down, what should my reaction be?

Often the excitement is short-lived. You know you are forgiven, but you are still trapped. The truth is, you'll continue to feel trapped until you put it into action, until you believe that you are forgiven

Start acting like a forgiven person, because the statement "I am forgiven" requires you to do something. In order to see results, spoken words must be backed by action.

For you it might include change of behavior, speech, association, dress, habits, etc. These changes will help you to embrace a lifestyle that affirms your new identity in Christ Jesus. Glory to GOD!

These three words, "I am forgiven," describe behavioral change. Behavioral change is a beginning of a new life, a life of daily experiences that are new. It is a life of GOD's way, not yours.

"For we are his workmanship, created in Christ Jesus unto good works, which GOD had before ordained that we should walk in them." (Ephesians 2:10)

All in all, it's about reclaiming your original identity. The phrase "I am forgiven" seeks for us to learn something. We need to agree with GOD.

Did I do something wrong?

These are internal conversations—nobody is with you but you.

As you begin to reclaim your identity and get excited about your new life, sometimes the internal conversations you have might sound like this:

It feels like all eyes are on me now.
Am I the subject of discussion?
Why does it feel like everybody is waiting to see my downfall?
How did they know?
Was it something I did or said?
Is change that visible or noticeable in my life?
I don't understand. Nobody seemed to care or notice me, but, all of a sudden, everybody wants to see whether I'll make it through.

The truth is, serving GOD sometimes comes with its own uncertainty. Sometimes you don't even know what to do. You feel like a sheep about to be slaughtered, but you continue to follow the shepherd—trustingly.

The renewed confidence you have in GOD will make you realize that there are things GOD is dealing with in you, things you didn't even know were inside you. Sometimes you'll feel like a spectator watching yourself transform. The unnerving part of it is that in such instances you don't hear the voice of GOD. It seems all quiet, like you're all alone. Yet, there are these people who are watching your every move.

It's confusing—sometimes you don't know what to do except seek the company of other Christians. You feel safe in that environment. You just want to surround yourself with like-minded people—Christians.

I guess GOD is talking even in that quiet moment, because you still know what to do. Daily you begin to realize that Christianity is not for the fainthearted:

"As the mountains surround Jerusalem, so the LORD surrounds his people—both now and forever more" (Psalm 125:2).

Even at that moment, you will feel surrounded too.

Understand this: forgiveness is not just for you

GOD is always kingdom-minded in the manner in which He deals with us. Even when it comes to forgiveness, I'm daily beginning to realize that GOD did not forgive me just for me. I need to forgive everyone who crosses my path.

How else will Christ be formed in them? GOD is kingdom-minded; He knows the hearts of these people, but still I must forgive them. GOD forgave me so I can forgive multitudes. Forgiveness is not for today's hurts but for tomorrow and future hurts. I must depend on His provision for each day. He will carry me through.

This is the love of GOD:

"For this reason I bow my knees before the Father, from whom every family in heaven and on earth derives its name, that He would grant you, according to the riches of His glory, to be strengthened with power through His Spirit in the inner man, so that Christ may dwell in your hearts through faith; and that you, being rooted and grounded in love, may be able to comprehend with all the saints *what is the breadth and length and height and depth, and to know the love of Christ which surpasses knowledge,* that you may be filled up to all the fullness of God." (Ephesians 3:14–19 NASB)

GOD does not want to see any of us perish. *None should perish but all be saved: this is His heartbeat.*

I need to remember that He is our Father—not just my father. He fathers all of us. He cares for all of us.

Since I am made in His image and after His likeness, I have got to imitate my Father in every respect.

six

Emotions We Go Through

Scenario 1

- **DO YOU KNOW WHAT YOU'RE ASKING OF ME? I CAN'T!**

Often, this is our reaction when asked to forgive. We say this when we have been hurt badly, and we feel justified in our decision not to forgive. The truth is, if it were easy, GOD would not ask you to forgive.

GOD tells us to forgive because what we're carrying is not physical but emotional. Yes, you've been hurt, and you're still hurting.
Can you show me where the pain is?
Is it something you can touch? Is it physical?
The answer is no!
But you're still leaking the wounds.

Healing must first be psychological before it can be physical.
When you decide to forgive, you release the pain. It will not go away overnight, but it will disappear gradually.

> *Any battle that is won in the spiritual realm is won com-
> pletely; the physical realm follows the spiritual!*

Scenario 2

I wish it were that simple...

You are born again, and it's been a couple of years now.

You relocated to another province and told yourself that your past is behind you. Things have been going well, and you have started to see the hand of GOD move mightily in your life. Even your love life is going well.

You are happy. You love GOD, and you enjoy the fellowship of your new church and your newfound family in Christ.

Everything is fine until, one day, you go to a grocery store, and you bump into someone from your past that once hurt you badly. You thought you were over the incident. You've moved on and believed you had healed, but now you look into this person's eyes, and suddenly your eyes are filled with rage.

Why has he followed you here? How can he do this to you? Has he not caused you enough pain? Why is he doing this to you?

Without a word, you run out and go home. You are upset, very upset. It feels like you are watching a movie. The past is back to haunt you.

As if that were not enough, on Sunday this person comes to your church, and when an altar call is made for those who want to repent, he goes in front to seek for forgiveness.

After church, he manages to get your attention and says, "Can you please forgive me?"

What do you say? Your mind says, "How dare he takes advantage of a situation where I'm forced to be polite to him?"

Instead, you ask him to meet with you, so you can talk privately.

Sitting at home, you start to question the wisdom of your decision. Shouldn't you have dealt with it at church, once and for all?

Is the waiting too much? Are you anxious? What's going on your mind? Are you having second thoughts about the meeting? Should you confide in someone from church? Or should you go with your boyfriend to the meeting?

Pain (in this context) is the outcome of a relationship gone wrong. What do you do?

What hurts me is not some argument I had with a stranger over a parking space. Yes, it upsets me, but it soon melts away, disappearing into thin air. Anyway, why should it bother me? I don't even know the person. Even if I were to see that person again, I would have forgotten the incident ever took place. It means nothing me.

The point I'm trying to make is that pain originates from close association. That's why you get all sorts of reactions from people when they're supposed to forgive. The unforgivable incident violated something very precious in them and caused so much unimaginable pain and turmoil inside.

You want to forgive. You want to move on, but you find it difficult. Where do you start? You need help. You can't go on.

Scenario 3

One person might say:

- I dread going home.
  Just thinking about it makes me upset, and the worst part is that every day this thing is staring me in the face. I can't hide myself from it. It's like it's out to destroy me, to bring me to nothing.

  I read the Bible, and it said I am a hypocrite when I act all righteous but fail to forgive the person I stay with. The problem is, it's not just one thing. Every day I discover how much this person is set to destroy me. He is a witch!

That's why I call him a witch. Do you think he is calling me names? I guess he is. Right now, I know we don't trust each other. There's too much pretense, but we both know that things have changed, and they have changed for the worse. We are not what we were hoping to find from each other. Maybe what is happening is that we have finally realized that we'll never become what we were hoping we'd become. We were all along buying time, hoping for a miracle. It never came. We are still what we were. I guess we were blinded by false hope, hope that will never be realized. Now, instead of talking about it honestly, we despise each other. We stay together, but we continue to build walls around ourselves.

This is not life! I'm happy when I'm alone, when I know he's not coming back. I'm happy to have the place to myself. I pray to GOD to help me buy myself my own house. I'm long past the rental stage.

Scenario 4

What about this one, who cries out and says:

- Help! This is too much.
  I'm trying, I really am, but it feels like the more I try, the more I fail. The problem is the person I'm expected to forgive stays in the same house as me.
  Yes, you are married to this person.
  For you, it might be a parent that has hurt you badly.
  You can't move out.

Where will you go? You are a minor or a wife who depends on this man.
So where do you start?

The monster is constantly in your face, and you say to forgive!
And you think, "It is not possible!"
But we can choose how we react.
We can vent all we want:
Shout at each other, throw things at each other, and say hurtful things, because we are hurting and are not thinking straight.
But, what does it achieve?

I'm not saying you should be calm about the situation.
But think before you speak. Remember: he who controls the mind controls you.

Unforgiveness has a hold on you. It has held you captive, and it's feeding on you.

You spend days on end thinking about revenge; you suffer from nightmares; you can't sleep at night. How long do you plan to go on like this?

Forgiveness is a lot more about you than the person who has caused you pain. The Bible encourages us to live at peace with one another. Unforgiveness breeds resentment, and resentment breeds bitterness. Bitterness kept inside can be very toxic, leading to countless opportunistic diseases that can be fatal.

So the next time you want to shout for help:

First empty this load you're carrying. Then, ask yourself if you still need to shout at all.

Forgiveness is a state of mind that says pain or hurt does not hurt anymore. Forgiveness is peace of mind. It's very liberating.

Can you see GOD's love for you? He deals with the worst so we can handle the rest.

There is saying: "Free your mind—free your soul." Even people who are unsaved understand that the trap is our refusal to let go.

Scenario 5

For you, it might be issues of trust, and you say:

- I don't trust anyone.
  There are things in our lives that are too embarrassing
  to talk about,
  Things you wish would be kept in the closet.
  If possible, no one should know about them.
  Or if they know, no one should ask you anything about
  it, because you don't want to go back there.

  You feel too ashamed, guilty, and stupid.
  The truth is, keeping it in the closet does not make it go
  away.
  In fact, when Satan is tired of your holier-than-thou
  attitude, he reminds you of your secret.
  It keeps you preoccupied, since you're always so careful
  not to let it out.
  Besides, what will people say? You seem to be an angel, someone who could never do wrong. You seem too clean.

  Maybe your excuse is not that you don't want people to
  know but that you've worked too hard to get to where
  you are, and you can't let anything or anyone mess it up
  for you. Can't you see, you'll forever be trapped, trapped
  by your past?
  Have you confessed, or is it still hounding you?
  It's time to let it all out. Just do it.
  The clock is ticking...you know what to do.

The Dalai Lama said:

"Our prime purpose in this life is to help others. And if you can't help them, at least don't hurt them." (BrainyQuote.com. "Dalai Lama quotes." Accessed April 27, 2013. http://www.brainyquote.com/quotes/d/dalailama158917.htm). The truth is that the very people who used to help us have now turned against us and are hurting us.

Hurt even as we feel we need to forgive—for our own sake. That is the whole point.

As you read this book, one thing I need you to understand very well is that forgiveness is a process.

There'll be days where you feel the load has been taken off your shoulder, and then something will happen that takes you back to that state of resentment. It's what you do that will determine how fast you heal. It is a process. Don't rush it or raise your expectations too high. Don't set yourself up for failure, because going forward, you'll establish how fast you heal. Remember, once you have decided to forgive, you begin to gain control again, especially over your emotions. Gradually, it will go away.

Now, you are in control. Don't give it away over minor setbacks along the way. It still hurts; you're still not over it. In fact, it seems like everyone is rubbing you the wrong way, waiting for you to explode. They can still see the pain in your eyes. It's there, no matter how hard you try to reassure everyone around you that you're fine. They can see you're not. The truth is you are not fine yet, but you are slowly recovering. They don't understand that work has already begun in earnest, internally.

You are well on your way...

seven

Unforgiveness Is a Stronghold

Most, if not all, people find it difficult to forgive.

Even after you have taken the first steps to forgiveness, it seems like there are things that continually want to hold you back.

You are happy for a moment and then upset the next minute, especially when something triggers the bad memories. Then you wallow in self-pity and allow all the floodgates of bad memories to overwhelm you all over again.

Suddenly you feel like you can't forgive, or could it be that you were fooling yourself when you said you are ready to put it all behind you? You are wrestling with your mind.

This person is not even there, but this feeling is so intense, it can't let you go.

You're in your room, and you feel like you are back where you started. It's an emotional rollercoaster, and it's playing you big time. This thing that refuses to let go is a stronghold.

A simple explanation of the word stronghold is this: anything that masters you has a potential stronghold on you. In his article, *"Battling Strongholds"* Jim Hammond has this to say:

> "It is easy to pull a weed; it is harder to pull a tree. When a thought process is incidental, it can be isolated and confronted,

or redirected, or removed, but when a thought process becomes entrenched, it is more difficult to remove. It has become a stronghold. There are some synonyms for this: addictions, habits, compulsive behaviors, just to name a few."

For though we live in the world, we do not wage war as the world does. The weapons we fight with are not the weapons of the world. On the contrary, they have divine power to demolish strongholds. We demolish arguments and every pretension that sets itself up against the knowledge of God, and we take captive every thought to make it obedient to Christ. **(2 Corinthians 10:3–5)**

Notice the last verse we read, 2 Corinthians 10:5. It speaks more about thought processes than it does about outward actions and behaviors.

Strongholds are internal problems, often external armor provides little safeguard over them. Because they are internal problems, an internal answer needs to be applied.

An effort to consistently avoid external sources of temptation by itself will be inadequate. The desires need to be cleansed internally and replaced by GOD's desires, GOD's disciplines, GOD's thoughts, and GOD's priorities and passions."

(Hammond, Jim. "Battling Strongholds." Accessed February 21, 2013. http://www.vvchristianchurchmedia. com/Articles/battling_strongholds.htm)

Talk to the Father. He remains the most dependable, reliable and available.
Speak to Him.

Dealing with the spiritual world

Healing is a spoken word as much as forgiveness is a spoken word, but the act manifests itself through behavioral change. That is why we talk about it. Before action can be taken, it must first be spoken. Can you see the power of the spoken word? Remember John 1:1 reads, "In the beginning was the Word, and the Word was with GOD and the Word was GOD." Verse 14 (a) reads: "and the Word became flesh and dwelt among us."

The Word creates, in as much as the Word has the power to destroy. There is so much power in the spoken word.

What controls the physical world is the spiritual!

As Christians, we need to understand that we experience forgiveness spiritually before it can be experienced physically.

An extract from Death and Afterward series *"Man a Trinity (Spirit, Soul, and Body)"* by Lehman Strauss:

> "Satan knows full well that he dominates the physical or the soulish man. Therefore he does not care if a man goes to a church where the Spirit of GOD is not in evidence. He knows that his victim is a creature of emotions, and it matters not if the emotions are stirred to sentimentalism or even to tears, just so long as man's spirit does not come in contact with GOD's Holy Spirit.
>
> Personally, I believe that Satan would rather have man go to a modernistic church, where there is false worship, than to a house of prostitution. *The soul is the seat of the passions, the feelings, and the desires of man, and Satan is satisfied if he can master these.* FW Grant, *one of Christianity's most honoured and respected Bible exponents (1834-1902) writes in his book "Facts and Theories*

as to a Future State", *Chapter 6:* "the soul is the seat of the affections, right or wrong, of love, hate, lusts, and even the appetites of the body."

Dr. James R. Graham (an Irish astrophysicist who works primarily in the fields of infrared astronomy instrumentation and adaptive optics) says that the main theater of the Holy Spirit's activity in man, and the part of man's nature with which He has peculiar affinity, is the spirit of man. The Apostle Paul gives us the Word of GOD on this, a passage that is sadly neglected. Isaiah 64:4 KJV, Paul wrote:

"But as it is written, Eye hath not seen, nor ear heard, neither have entered into the heart of man, the things which GOD hath prepared for them that love Him."

A great many people stop here, content to remain in ignorance. However, Paul continues:

But God hath revealed them unto us by His Spirit; for the Spirit searcheth all things, yea, the deep things of God.

As we learn in 1 Corinthians 2:9–11, "For what man knoweth the things of a man, save the spirit of man which is in him? Even so the things of God knoweth no man, but the Spirit of God."

The Bible says; "There is a spirit in man; and the inspiration of the Almighty giveth them understanding" (Job 32:8). Here we are told that it is the spirit of man that is given understanding. The materialist tells us that the spirit of man is the air that he breathes, and that man's body is all there is to his personality. Such is not the case.

The spirit of man is his personality, and it is that which differentiates him from the lower animal creation.

If "spirit" meant merely "breath," GOD certainly would not deal with it as a personality. He is called "The God of the spirits of all flesh" (Numbers 16:22), and "the Father of spirits" (Hebrews 12:9). It is by His spirit that the Christian both serves and worships GOD. Paul testified: "For God is my witness, Whom I serve with my spirit in the Gospel" (Romans 1:9). Jesus said: "God is a spirit; and they that worship Him must worship Him in spirit and in truth" (John 4:24)."

(Strauss, Lehman. "Man a Trinity (Spirit, Soul and Body)" Death and Afterward Series, June 14, 2004. Accessed May 3, 2013. https://bible.org/seriespage/man-trinity-spirit-soul-body.)

eight

Challenges Along the Way...

It's easy to deal with challenges from people who are not born again and also from people who are not your family, but when these are the people you need to forgive, it becomes a different ball game altogether.

The other day, I was coming from an event that had gone wrong. I had been part of the committee that organized the event. So I came back home, made myself something to eat, and slept. I wanted to sleep the event away and forget that it even happened.

When I woke up, it was 09:40 p.m., and I remembered that I had only wanted to take a nap and go to the all-night prayer service. So I was looking at the clock and deciding whether I should go or just put on my pajamas (since I had fallen asleep with my clothes on) and go back to sleep.

Just then I thought, *No way! I am still going.* I got myself ready, and I was out at 10:00 p.m. I enjoyed myself and came back in the early hours of the morning. Instead of going to sleep, I started to pray as the Holy Spirit led me. I prayed for over an hour while the Holy Spirit kept showing me what I needed to pray about.

Eventually I turned off the light and slept. I was still partially awake when I noticed a figure of a person I know coming into my room. This person did not come in physical form, but I saw the spirit body.

This figure came close, as if to feed me something, and –it touched my mouth. I fought hard, and GOD gave me victory. Then something, which looked like a scary beast, walked into my room in spirit form. This beast was big, and GOD again gave me victory over this beast.

I was so thankful, and I continued to thank GOD. Eventually, I fell asleep. The following day, I noticed the funny look the person gave me.

He fights for me!

Psalm 124:2-3 ESV reads: "If it had not been for the LORD who was on our side when people rose up against us, then they would have swallowed us up alive." Psalm 124:6–7 reads: "Blessed be the LORD, who has not given us as prey to their teeth! We have escaped like a bird from the snare of the fowlers; the snare is broken we have escaped!"

This is what happened: GOD saved me.

Now, the challenge is the strong resentment I developed toward this person and the lack of trust I have toward those over whom GOD has made me victorious.

These people I see very often. The Bible commands me to forgive. Honestly, I wanted to see GOD wipe them out for good. I felt justified in my request, because it is not just one wrong they have committed toward me. It's like they are continually on the warpath to destroy me. It is too much.

This was until I had a discussion with a pastor who also happens to be my colleague. He told me to pray for them and plead their cases before GOD. He told me that even Jesus prayed for his enemies and loves them. I am also expected to pray for them and love them.

In the evening, before I went to sleep, I prayed for them and suddenly I felt something lift off my shoulders. In fact I started to pray at our evening prayer session, praising GOD for His faithfulness.

I must say, I slept well—peaceful.

Anger is heavy; it is heavy in one's soul. I know it, and I don't want it anymore. I don't want any heavy load. Hlengiwe Mhlaba, the renowned

South African Gospel artist who sings the song "heavy load", knows what I'm talking about. I don't want it; it is toxic!

Dealing with the present.
Is this true?
Do you know why people cheat and lie?
Because they know it's easier to get forgiveness than permission.
I also heard someone say: Only trust someone who can see these three things in you:

- The sorrow behind your smile
- The love behind your anger
- The reason behind your silence

Now, based on the first statement, are Christians being taken advantage of?
As a Christian, do you find that people expect you to automatically forgive them? Do you feel taken advantage of? Who is willing to empathize with you?
Or could it be that we seek too much empathy and self-justification?
How can you tell if people are sincere when seeking forgiveness?
What then becomes the point of forgiveness?

What if it's Christian-to-Christian?
What is your reaction to forgiveness when someone is a fellow Christian, a spouse, a friend, a child?
Can you look that person in the eye and say, "I know the devil tempted you, and I forgive you completely"?
Can you still find love behind your anger toward the person?
Could it be that you're still filled with sorrow behind your smile?

How genuine are people when they seek your forgiveness?
Do they show remorse? Do you feel they are sincere?
What about issues of trust?

Counseling in the church?

Will you suggest counseling? Who offers counseling in your church? Do you feel you can open up to them? Is the church well equipped to deal with issues of unforgiveness?

Are there members in your own church who are walking around with open wounds? Are there people who are bleeding in secret? How can we help?

Or could it be that we don't want to get involved? If we turn a blind eye, where must they run to? What must be the role of the church?

Again, when it's Christian-to-Christian, what happens afterward?

Do you continue to fellowship in the same church?

Do you continue to serve like you used to?

How does the church handle splinter groups or cliques in the church? Haven't we been warned about division in the church?

These people (splinter groups and cliques) don't plan to leave the church—they all love GOD.

Is the church well equipped to handle such matters?

Are the existing structures and channels effective?

Are we afraid to discuss such matters for fear of isolation? Are we afraid of being removed from the church board and stripped of our duties?

nine

What Is the Lesson?

The Oxford English Dictionary defines forgiveness as "to grant free pardon and to give up all claim on account of an offense or debt."

Forgiveness may be considered simply in terms of the person who forgives, in terms of the person forgiven, or in terms of the relationship between the forgiver and the person forgiven.

People who have been forgiven of grave wrongdoing truly know how precious forgiveness is. They are careful not to mess up and are always eager to please so as to maintain a healthy relationship. This behavior carries on for some time, until the person feels he has done enough to pay for the wrong and resorts to his old ways.

Wrongdoing/evil is a human trait, generously spread among all men and women. It infects everyone. As long as imperfection exists, people will only succeed in replacing one evil with another, although some evils are more tolerable than others.

Do we ever learn?

Yes, but often it is a process. What keeps the person from wrongdoing is the desire to change. Mary Fairchild writes on the Internet "What Does the Bible Say About Forgiveness?" frequently asked questions about forgiveness in the Bible, and says:

"I believe forgiveness is a choice we make through a decision of our will, motivated by obedience to God and his command to forgive.

The desire to change can never be superficial; it must be genuine.

Can I take advantage of it?

No. It's precious, treat it that way. It's Christ who is at work in you to transform you into His likeness—what you're predestined to become.

Let go—learn to forgive

Today, some people get hospitalized because of bitterness They refuse to forgive. They harbor anger, pain, frustration, rejection, and they refuse to let go. They justify their anger by telling themselves that what was done to them is unforgiveable. Their hearts grow cold by day, unable to forgive, and in the process they grow even more miserable. Why? It's simply because they refuse to let go.

Be gentle and forbearing with one another and, if one has a difference (a grievance or complaint) against another, readily pardoning each other; even as the Lord has [freely] forgiven you, so must you also [forgive]. (Colossians 3:13 AMP)

Did you see the word "readily"? It means you purpose in your heart to forgive. "Readily" means easily or without any difficulty.

How do we forgive when we don't feel like it? How do we translate the decision to forgive into a change of heart?

Mary Fairchild continues to say, "We forgive by faith, out of obedience. Since forgiveness goes against our nature, we must forgive by faith, whether we feel like it or not. We must trust God to do the work in us that needs to be done so that the forgiveness will be complete."

I believe GOD honors our commitment to obey Him and our desire to please Him when we choose to forgive. He completes the work in His time. We must continue to forgive (our job), by faith, until the work of forgiveness (the Lord's job), is done in our hearts.

And I am certain that GOD, who began the good work within you, will continue His work until it is finally finished on the day when Christ Jesus returns. (Philippians 1:6 NLT)"

(Fairchild, Mary. "What Does the Bible Say About Forgiveness?" Frequently asked questions about forgiveness. About.com, New York Times. Accessed June 15, 2013, http://christianity.about.com/od/whatdoesthebiblesay/a/bibleforgiveness.htm.)

Forgiveness is a transformed mind—in phases

As I write this book, I began to realize that when GOD gave me this title, *"I Am Forgiven"*, He was telling me I needed to more thoroughly understand what it means to be forgiven by GOD.

Sometimes I walk around and wonder: does a forgiven person behave like me?

Why do I still have these thoughts? Am I ungrateful? Don't I realize what GOD did for me? Why does it feel like I sometimes intend to do wrong?

Some days are better than others. Some days, I walk around feeling good, feeling that my life is really beginning to shape up and that I'm ready to go out and make it big. I'm driven; I'm alive!

That was till yesterday

I'll give you a new slogan to adopt. It goes like this:
"That was till yesterday." You are in control now.

Forgive and move on

It's funny how most of the time we claim to have forgiven others only to have expectations.
We call in favors, sometimes make unreasonable demands, and don't expect to be turned down. Can we honestly call this forgiveness? Certainly not! This is bargaining
In forgiveness there are no trade-offs—you simply forgive and move on.
Forgiveness does not ask: "What can you offer me?" This is wrong, and it must stop!

ten

Set Your Own Pace

Over and above every book that has ever been written about forgiveness, what you need to learn is that each one of us has a different way of dealing with it, saved or not. The advantage you have when you are born-again is that the Holy Spirit is there with you, all the way, to help you heal.

You don't have to attend a series of appointments with a clinical psychologist to talk it out (no offense to the professionals); you don't even have to attend a number of counseling sessions in your home church. Over and above everything else, you need to stay in sync with the Holy Spirit to guide you through.

Remember, we said forgiveness is a process. After you have talked about it, sought counseling, and agreed to move on, remember the pain will not disappear just like that because you said so. It will require for you to work it out of your system.

What was violated was not something that was built or established overnight, so getting you back together again will take a lot from you.

If your well-being matters to you that much, then you need to get started. Set your own pace; don't try to avoid these emotions when you get all worked up. You need to deal with them, one at a time. Be sensitive to the guidance of the Holy Spirit. Sometimes what you hear might not agree with what you feel, but if you're serious about getting out of this state, you'll have to make the move.

The Holy Spirit is gentle and will never set you up for failure.

Greater is He that is within me than the devil that is in the world.
Fight when dealing with your persecutors.
Forgiveness is free, but to stay forgiven is a battle, so *fight!*

Now that you're forgiven, you need to fight to stay forgiven.

There is an opponent who's forever plotting your downfall. Let's look at these two words carefully, a contender and a title holder.

What is an opponent?

An opponent is someone who competes against or fights another in a contest, game, or argument.

An opponent is someone who has gone to great lengths to learn as much as possible about the title holder. He or she has had it done over a period of time to prepare for the take-over. On the day of the contest, the opponent comes to do nothing but to finish you off. The only concern is the trophy/prize, and will do whatever it takes to win.

These are the daily struggles you encounter. Just because you are forgiven doesn't mean the devil will step aside and applaud. He will fight you. He is your opponent.

Imagine this: you have decided that you will begin to tithe. The devil will watch you once, but the second time around, he will wage war. The devil will use every trick to prevent you from putting your money into that offering basket. As soon as the month is over, or even before, things will start to fall apart. You will start to worry and panic, and at that moment the only money you have will be your tithe. What do you do?

Without giving it a second thought, you take the money and use it. The devil will laugh at you—he knows he's got you right where he wants you. Unless you fight, he's won you over. You will become yet another conquest, excited he celebrates your downfall. You're frustrated. You feel bad about it; you feel like you can't cope. The worst part is that as the months progress, you can't account for your money, and the situation is not getting any better. What do you do?

Who is this person who's doing all this to you? It is your opponent. He is consumed by this fighting spirit. He's determined to take you out for good.

What is a title holder?

A title holder is someone who has legitimate documents that prove ownership. It is someone who is on the throne.

The English dictionary talks about someone who has won first place in a competition. In this context, you came in first place when you decided to give your life to Jesus as the LORD and Savior. You were given a new name, a new title. You are now called a child of GOD.

This is your title, and because of this, your contender envies you. Every now and then, the title holder forgets how precious his title is. He or she forgets or is unaware that she is being monitored constantly, which means the contender has access to the title holder. Often, it comes in a form of someone close.

The opponent is constantly plotting the title holder's downfall. The title holder is oblivious to the plot until something happens to alert the title holder. Once awakened to the opponent's attack, the title holder will want to fight back.

As a title holder, you deal with the hard blows and develop an approach that will help you rise again. Now, you need to fight a good fight. Fight a good fight of faith. It will require training and learning new approaches. At first it will be difficult, and you feel like giving up. It looks impossible, but you need to persist. Ignore the setbacks; ignore the pain; ignore the frustration; and focus on the goal. Remember, you cannot loose.

It's a fight, and whoever has the winning attitude conquers.

Remember, this is not simply a one-time battle. You will have to come up with new approaches constantly as the Holy Spirit guides you. *Fight!*

He is watching you.
Don't get too comfortable, or you might be caught napping.
Stay alert. Stay awake.
You are not alone.
GOD is on your side and at work within you.
Take courage!

The call to endurance:

> Therefore, since we also have such a large cloud of witnesses surrounding us, let us lay aside every weight and the sin that so easily ensnares us. Let us run with endurance the race that lies before us, keeping our eyes on Jesus, the source and perfecter of our faith, who for the joy that lay before Him endured a cross and despised the shame and has sat down at the right hand of God's throne. (Hebrews 12: 1–2 HCSB)

It's not about how I feel but embracing the truth.

In my life, I've noticed how sometimes I try so hard to do right, as though I'm trying to qualify for forgiveness.

I want to do well. There is nothing wrong with pleasing GOD but not as form of bargain. He forgave me not as form of bargain.

He forgave me not by my works but *grace* alone. Proverbs 23:23 HCSB reads: "Buy and do not sell truth, wisdom, instruction, and understanding."

The truth is GOD forgave me. I need GOD's wisdom every step of the way to understand this and how to make it work for me. I don't need to think about justification. I need to constantly obey GOD's instruction and carry it out so that I can acquire understanding.

Sometimes condemnation shows its ugly face and begins to plant seeds of doubt in our minds. If we're not careful and we're not rooted in the Word (reading and applying it in our daily circumstances), we might find ourselves believing a lie. This is what Satan wants to do: detach us from the Word and fellowship as we begin to see ourselves as failures. We need the Word to constantly reassure ourselves of our identities.

Living a life of forgiveness is living a life filled with gratitude, not out of indebtedness but endless devotion to GOD.

A forgiven person is silent before GOD even when there are raging storms from all sides.

Silence is not absence of words but confidence in GOD's divine intervention.

It's about a relationship of trust and honesty that says He is my shelter and my comfort—I am safe in Him.

It does not mean that nothing will ever go wrong.
It does not mean that you will stop experiencing setbacks.

It teaches one single-mindedness.
It is concerned about building a lasting relationship.
It does not make any false promises.

Forgiveness is the ability to prosper so that you are able to say:
"I will leave to see the greatness of my name realized to the glory of the most high GOD!"

In the path of wellness, there will be many boring days.

Many days will be full of nothing but responsibility,

self-discipline,and hard work.

GOD bless...

A Prayer of Repentance

A Prayer of Emotional Repentance: Putting Off My Old Mood States

"Father, I've sinned against You by worshipping feelings instead of worshipping You.

My current mood state of _______ exposes how desperately I'm trying to live without You.

My failure to face my feelings exposes my distrust in Your ability to care for me.

My refusal to soothe my soul in You exposes my doubts about Your goodness.

I put off my emotional duplicity replacing it, in the power of Your Spirit, with emotional integrity.

I will face whatever I feel and bring it to You. I put off my emotional lasciviousness.

I put off indulging my fleshly passions. I confess as sin my addiction to _________.

I recognize it for what it is: a symptom of the deeper disorder within me, a spiritual, relational, mental, and willful disorder.

Forgive me. Empower me to manage my moods for Your glory and the good of others."

(Kellemen, Bob. "Six Prayers of Repentance." RPM Ministries, September 20, 2011, http://www.rpmministries.org/2011/09/six-prayers-of-repentance/)

Prayer of Confession and Pardon

Prayers of Confession and Pardon

O Holy One, we call to you and name you as eternal, ever-present, and boundless in love. Yet there are times, O God, when we fail to recognize you in the dailyness of our lives. Sometimes shame clenches tightly around our hearts, and we hide our true feelings. Sometimes fear makes us small, and we miss the chance to speak from our strength. Sometimes doubt invades our hopefulness, and we degrade our own wisdom.

Holy God, in the daily round from sunrise to sunset, remind us again of your holy presence hovering near us and in us. Free us from shame and self-doubt. Help us to see you in the moment-by-moment possibilities to live honestly, to act courageously, and to speak from our wisdom.

Dear Heavenly Father, we lower our heads before you, and we confess that we have too often forgotten that we are yours. Sometimes we carry on our lives as if there was no God and we fall short of being a credible witness to You. For these things we ask your forgiveness and we also ask for your strength. Give us clear minds and open hearts so we may witness to You in our world. Remind us to be who You would have us to be regardless of what we are doing or who we are with. Hold us to You and build our relationship with You and with those You have given us on earth.

Almighty and most merciful Father, we have erred and strayed from Your ways like lost sheep. We have followed too much the devices and desires of our own hearts. We have offended against Your holy laws. We have left undone those things which we ought to have done; and we have done those things which we ought not to have done; and there is nothing good in us. O Lord, have mercy upon us, miserable offenders. Spare those, O God, who confess their faults. Restore those who are penitent; according to Your promises declared unto men in Christ Jesus our Lord. Grant that we may hereafter live a godly, righteous, and sober life; to the glory of His name. Amen

---

Almighty God, who does freely pardon all who repent and turn to Him, now fulfil in every contrite heart the promise of redeeming grace; forgiving all our sins, and cleansing us from an evil conscience; through the perfect sacrifice of Christ Jesus our Lord. Amen.

(Presbyterian Church. 1946. "The Book of Common Worship." USA: Westminster John Knox Press)

Acronyms

AMP: Amplified Version Bible

ESV: English Standard Version Bible

HCSB: Holman Christian Standard Bible

KJV: King James Version Bible

NASB: New American Standard Bible

NKJV: New King James Version Bible

NLT: New Living Translation Bible

References

BrainyQuote.com. "Dalai Lama quotes." Accessed April 27, 2013. http://www.brainyquote.com/quotes/quotes/d/dalailama158917.htm

Fairchild, Mary. "What Does the Bible Say About Forgiveness?" Frequently asked questions about forgiveness. About.com. The New York Times Company. Accessed June 15, 2013. http://christianity.about.com/od/whatdoesthebiblesay/a/bibleforgiveness.htm

Grant, F.W. 1889. "Facts and Theories as to a Future State." Functions and relationships of soul and spirit. 2nd Edition.   Harvard University. http://www.neble.co.uk/grant/Facts/chapter6.html

Hammond, Jim. "Battling Strongholds." Accessed February 21, 2013. http//www.vvchristianchurchmedia.com/Articles/battling_strongholds.htm

Hebron's Mexico Missions. "Equipping Faithful Disciples." Who should be equipped for the ministry? Accessed July 13, 2013 http://www.equipsaints.org/equip1.htm

Kellemen, B. "Six Prayers of Repentance." RPM Ministries, September 20, 2011, http://www.rpmministries.org/2011/09/six-prayers-of-repentance/

Presbyterian Church. 1946. "Book of Common Worship." USA: Westminster John Knox Press.

Strauss, Lehman. "Man a Trinity (Spirit, Soul and Body)." Death and Afterward Series, June 14, 2004, Accessed May 30, 2013, https://bible.org/seriespage/man-trinity-spirit-soul-body

Yeakley Jr, Flavil R. 1979. "Why Churches Grow." Plainview: Christian Communications Inc.

Glory

be

to

GOD

www.ingramcontent.com/pod-product-compliance
Lightning Source LLC
Chambersburg PA
CBHW071509030726
47593CB00003B/1240